Who Was
Harvey Milk?

by Corinne Grinapol

illustrated by Gregory Copeland

Penguin Workshop

For everyone working to repair the world—CG

For Patty and Larae—GC

PENGUIN WORKSHOP
An Imprint of Penguin Random House LLC, New York

Visit us online at www.penguinrandomhouse.com.

Library of Congress Control Number: 2019054768

ISBN 9781524792787 (paperback)   10 9 8 7 6 5 4 3 2 1
ISBN 9781524792794 (library binding)   10 9 8 7 6 5 4 3 2 1

Contents

Who Was Harvey Milk?

During the final years of the Great Depression, when Harvey Milk was about eight or nine, he loved going to the movies. On many Saturdays, he would spend his allowance on tickets to the local movie theater. All across the country, there were special Saturday-afternoon shows with movies just for kids. But the movies weren't the reason Harvey liked going.

Raffles were held during the daytime movies, making it possible for kids to win prizes if the number on their ticket was chosen. Harvey went to the movies always hoping that his ticket would win him a prize. But it wasn't really the prize that he wanted.

The prizes—things like watches and toy guns—were handed out onstage. The winners would come up to the stage to pick up whatever prize they had won. Although many winners probably did that quickly and quietly, Harvey did not.

When he'd win, Harvey would make a show out of it, taking low, dramatic bows and getting the packed crowd of kids in the theater to cheer him on. That is what Harvey looked forward to most: the cheers and the attention he received when he was on the stage.

After Harvey grew up, he still loved to perform in front of people. He wanted them to pay attention to what he had to say. But grown-up Harvey wasn't an actor. Instead, he ran for public office, using his talent and skills to inspire others, to fight for the rights of all people, and to try to change his community for the better. This is his story.

CHAPTER 1
The Milks Come to Woodmere

Harvey Bernard Milk was born on May 22, 1930, in Woodmere, New York, a town on Long Island about an hour from New York City. The first person in Harvey Milk's family to come to Woodmere was his grandfather, Mausche Milch. Mausche was born in what is now Lithuania, a country in northern Europe. He had a big family,

LITHUANIA

Long Island, New York

Atlantic Ocean

and it was hard to find work that could support his wife and five children. So he left on his own to find work in the United States.

Mausche was the only Jewish person in Woodmere, and he changed his name to Morris Milk to fit in more. He worked as a door-to-door salesman, selling things like clothes and fabric, called dry goods. He saved his money and opened his own store, Milk's Dry Goods.

The store did well, and after almost six years alone, it was time for the rest of Morris's family to come to America. His children changed their names in America, too. The youngest child, Hieke, became known as William. William was Harvey's father.

William, who called himself Bill, married Minerva "Minnie" Karns in 1925, when he was twenty-eight. Minnie's family was also Jewish and originally from Lithuania, too. Minnie had grown up in Brooklyn, New York. She was independent and funny, and she believed that women could do many of the same things men could. Bill and Minnie had two children, Robert Milk, born in 1926, and Harvey, born four years later.

By the time Robert and Harvey were born, Milk's Dry Goods had grown into Milk's Department Store. Harvey's grandfather became an important man in the community, which by then included a lot more Jewish people. He wanted to use his own wealth to give something back. In 1928, Morris and other leaders in Woodmere started a synagogue—a Jewish house of worship. They called it Congregation Sons of Israel.

Harvey grew up going to synagogue with his family. The leaders of the synagogue wanted its members to follow the traditional rules of their faith. They didn't work or use cars and other machines on the Sabbath—Saturday—the Jewish day of rest.

Harvey's mother wasn't strict about all the rules, but there was one important Jewish idea that Minnie believed in. It was called *tikkun olam*, which means to help fix the world.

For Minnie, that meant always being involved
in volunteer projects, like helping to feed the
poor. His mother's efforts to help others set an
important example for Harvey.

CHAPTER 2
Discoveries

Harvey Milk was an unusual-looking kid. He had big eyes, a big nose, and ears that stuck out from his head. Other children teased him, but Harvey just brushed off their taunts. Sometimes, he would tease them right back. Harvey was outgoing. He liked to make people laugh, and he loved to be the center of attention. In 1941, when eleven-year-old Harvey was at a party for a baby cousin, someone filmed the celebration. When the camera was on Harvey, who knew he was being filmed, his smile got wider and his eyes twinkled. He really enjoyed being in front of the camera.

Harvey had a lot of energy, and was even a bit of a troublemaker. From a young age,

he liked to pull pranks on friends and family members, just as his older brother did. Once, while their mother was at the store, Harvey and  Robert took all the labels off the canned goods in the house. After that, the only way for their mother to find out what was in the cans was to open them!

Harvey was really close with his grandfather Morris. He respected him for the work he did in their community, and he looked to him for advice. Harvey never forgot one of his grandfather's sayings: "Don't hide your green hair; people will see it anyway." He was letting Harvey know that he shouldn't try to cover up who he was. It was his grandfather's way of saying "Always be yourself."

Harvey's grandfather was a role model for him. And because his family was involved in the synagogue started by his grandfather, Harvey had his bar mitzvah at Sons of Israel when he was thirteen. A bar mitzvah (or bat mitzvah, for girls) is a Jewish ceremony that signals when a young person must begin to observe the Jewish commandments. They become responsible for their actions and behave more like adults within their religious community.

By the time of Harvey's bar mitzvah, however, he wasn't interested in the religious parts of Judaism. He didn't like all the rules synagogue members were supposed to follow, and he didn't like being told what to do. He was, however, proud of being a Jewish person.

Harvey grew up in the 1930s and 1940s, a time when there was a lot of anti-Semitism— discrimination against and sometimes hatred of Jews. There was even anti-Semitism on Long Island, where Harvey and his family lived. Many people traveled in the summer to the town of Yaphank, where marches were held for the Nazi Party and there was actually a street named for Adolf Hitler.

Cultural vs. Religious Judaism

When people say they're Jewish, they're not always talking about the religion of Judaism. The Old Testament is a religious book that both tells the story of the Jewish people and also describes the specific beliefs of their religion.

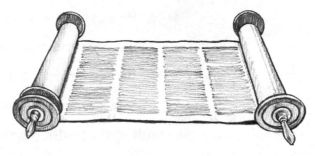

Many Jews choose to focus on their history instead of the Jewish religion. People who identify as culturally Jewish are interested in their family heritage and participating in the traditions of Judaism, but they may not attend services or be interested in thinking about the role of God in Judaism.

World War II and the Holocaust

Adolf Hitler, the leader of the Nazi Party in Germany, became the head of Germany's government in 1933. He was a dictator who had total control over the country. Hitler told Germans that all their problems were the fault of the Jewish people. His government committed violence against Jews and destroyed their businesses.

In 1939, Germany invaded the country of Poland. This marked the beginning of World War II. Soon, more countries would become involved, including the United States in 1941.

As the war continued, Hitler began an effort to kill all Jewish people. The persecution and murder of the Jews became known as the Holocaust. Hitler forced Jews in Germany and the countries he invaded to live in specific areas, called ghettos; they were eventually moved into concentration camps. By the end of the war in 1945, more than six million Jews had been killed, as well as about six million people from other groups, including Soviet citizens, Poles, Romani, and gay people from many countries.

In 1943, just before his bar mitzvah, Harvey learned about the Jews in the Warsaw ghetto in Poland. When they found out they were going to be sent to concentration camps, the Jews in Warsaw decided to fight the Nazis instead of going willingly. They fought bravely, but the Nazis eventually captured most of them, and they were sent to the camps.

The lessons of the Warsaw ghetto and the Holocaust stayed with Harvey. He believed it was important to fight for what you believe in. He also believed it was important to make the choice to do the right thing. And he never hid the fact that he was Jewish.

When he was fourteen, Harvey convinced his mother that he was old enough to go to New York City by himself to see the opera. Harvey had become an opera fan when he was just eleven. On Saturday afternoons, he would listen on the radio to performances by the Metropolitan Opera in New York. He'd move his arms around, pretending he was the conductor.

Harvey's mother gave him money for tickets in the standing-room section of the opera house. He traveled there by train. In the city, Harvey discovered many different types of people. He recognized that some of the men in the audience

were attending the opera together. They were similar to him in a specific way. Harvey realized that, like them, he was gay—that he was a young man who was attracted to other men. He was not yet ready, however, to let others know how he felt.

CHAPTER 3
School Days

In 1944, a fire almost completely destroyed Milk's Department Store. Officials believe the fire may have been started on purpose, possibly because Morris was Jewish. If that was the case, however, the guilty person was never found.

Morris rebuilt the store, but Harvey's father decided he wasn't going back to work there. In 1945, when Harvey was fifteen, the family moved to the town of Bay Shore, also on Long Island. Bill started his own business selling furs.

Harvey went to Bay Shore High School. There weren't a lot of Jews in the town, and sometimes the Jewish kids weren't invited to parties. But that didn't stop Harvey from making friends. It helped that he liked to clown around and make people laugh. Harvey was on the basketball team and junior varsity football team. He also wrestled and ran track. Even though Harvey was popular, he wanted to get through high school quickly. He was seventeen when he graduated in June 1947.

Harvey was in a rush to get out of high school, but he didn't know what he was rushing to get to. His parents suggested he go to the New York State College for Teachers at Albany. Harvey followed his parents' advice, and he started college that fall in the center of New York State. He studied math and history. He also tried to study languages but didn't do well in either French or German. He had picked them because they were the languages of the operas he so loved.

Harvey kept himself busy during his years at college. He wasn't a good enough athlete to make the school teams, but he became involved in intramural sports, with different teams of Albany students competing against one another. Harvey competed in football, soccer, volleyball, basketball, wrestling, and track. And he didn't just *play* sports. Harvey also coached a basketball team during his junior year—and it won!

Most of his classmates at the time dressed in button-down shirts, sweaters, and neatly pressed pants. But Harvey dressed like an athlete, wearing gray sweatpants, a gray sweatshirt, and sneakers around campus. To complete his athletic image, he joined the newspaper staff his sophomore year to write about sports.

Later, Harvey began writing articles about other topics for the paper. He supported student groups that faced discrimination. For example, Harvey believed that the white- and Christian-only fraternities and sororities, social groups of men and women on campus, should admit people of other races and religions. When one sorority

changed its rules to allow black women to join, Harvey congratulated the sorority in an article he wrote about the decision.

And even though Harvey joined the Jewish fraternity Kappa Beta, he told his fraternity brothers that they should let non-Jewish students in, too. Harvey hadn't joined  the fraternity for religious reasons, and the fraternity didn't focus on religion. So he didn't understand why non-Jewish students should be excluded.

Just as he had clowned around in high school, Harvey loved to act goofy and make people laugh in college. He made friends easily.

Harvey also liked the idea of having an important role at his college. But there was one area of campus life in which he wasn't successful: running for office. When he ran for freshman class president, he finished in fourth place out of five. He then ran to become treasurer of the athletic association, but he lost that race, too. When he tried to join one of the school's honor societies, he wasn't chosen as a member.

Even though Harvey had lost more than one election, he kept trying. Determination would play an important role in his future.

CHAPTER 4
From the Navy to the Classroom

Harvey had gone to a teachers college, so it would have made sense for him to get a teaching job after graduating in 1951. But he wasn't sure that teaching was what he wanted to do. On top of that, the Korean War had recently broken out. So upon graduating, Harvey decided to join the navy and fight in the war.

Not everyone who joined, or enlisted, was sent to Korea to fight. Because Harvey was a college graduate, he was sent to Officer Candidate School. At the navy's Newport, Rhode Island, campus, he and other young men were taught not just how to become sailors but also how to become the navy's future leaders. At the school, Harvey discovered he really liked deep-sea diving. His athletic skills helped make him good at it. Soon, he was a diving officer on the USS *Kittiwake*— a submarine rescue ship. If a submarine sank, the rescue ship's divers would plunge deep into the ocean to save stranded crewmen.

In 1953, Harvey was sent to a naval base in San Diego, California. During the years the United States fought in World War II, there were many sailors who lived for a time in cities like San Diego, where the navy had set up bases. Even though they had to keep it a secret, some of the sailors were gay. With more gay people living in some port cities, communities of gay people grew.

Being in San Diego opened up a whole new world for Harvey. By the time he arrived, he was able to choose from a number of gay bars where he could meet other men like him during his free time. But just because those places existed didn't mean visiting them was always safe. Police would sometimes storm into gay bars and arrest the patrons.

"Don't Ask, Don't Tell"

The ban—both official and unofficial—on gay people serving in the military goes back to the Revolutionary War. And from 1917 to 2011, the military had strict rules that kept gay people from serving.

In 1993, President Bill Clinton signed the "Don't Ask, Don't Tell" policy. It stated that the military simply wouldn't ask its members whether they were gay. However, if they came out—the term for openly living as a gay person—or were discovered to be gay, they would be discharged (let go from the military). That came to an end in September 2011, when the "Don't Ask, Don't Tell" policy was repealed. Openly gay and lesbian people could then serve in the military.

Harvey looked good in his navy uniform, and he knew it. He even wore his white officer uniform to his brother's wedding. In particular, he loved the belt, with a brass buckle that identified him as a diver. Years later, when he was no longer in the navy, he still wore the belt.

Harvey spent four years in the navy and was honorably discharged in August 1955. He had been named as a lieutenant junior grade and had won a number of awards, including the National Defense Service Medal and the Navy Good Conduct Medal.

When Harvey left the navy, he wasn't sure what he wanted to do next. He stayed in California for a while, heading north to Los Angeles. There he met and fell in love with John Harvey, and together they moved to Miami, Florida. When they broke up, Harvey moved back to New York and got an apartment in Queens, Long Island.

At the age of twenty-six, Harvey finally became what he had studied to become: a teacher. He got a job at George W. Hewlett High School, less than a ten-minute car ride from his hometown of Woodmere.

One summer day in 1956, before he started teaching, Harvey met Joe Campbell at Riis Park Beach in Queens. They started dating, and soon they were in a serious relationship.

Joe moved in with Harvey. Gay people weren't allowed to get married in the 1950s, but Harvey called their relationship a marriage.

Although Harvey didn't tell his family that he was gay or that he and Joe were living together, his mother seemed to realize that they were more than just friends. When Joe and Harvey came to visit, Minnie would talk about how skinny

Joe was, and make him meals. She also gave Joe presents. Once, Minnie knit a blanket and slippers for him—exactly like the ones she had knit for Harvey.

At Hewlett High, Harvey taught math and history to tenth- and eleventh-graders, and he coached the basketball team. Harvey was a popular teacher. He knew how to make kids laugh, and he could talk to them about things they were interested in, especially sports.

Even though he was good at teaching, Harvey wasn't sure he wanted to be a teacher for the rest of his life.

At that time, if a teacher was even suspected of being gay, he or she could be fired, and never allowed to teach again. Harvey didn't want to take that risk. He spent only one year as a teacher. After that, he was ready to move again. Harvey and Joe packed a car and drove to their new lives in Dallas, Texas.

CHAPTER 5
Heading West

Harvey and Joe spent less than a year in Dallas before moving back to New York. While there wasn't much keeping them in Dallas, there was something pulling them back to New York: Minnie had had a heart attack.

Harvey eventually got a job working at an insurance company. It paid well, and he and Joe were able to live in an apartment right across the street from Central Park, a huge park in the middle of Manhattan filled with lakes, grassy fields, trees, and trails. Harvey got them season tickets to the ballet and opera, and bought a pet toucan named Bill.

In 1961, Harvey and Joe broke up. They had

been together for five years. Harvey would never again have a relationship that lasted as long.

A year later, there was more bad news for Harvey. His mother had had another heart attack and died. It was 1962, and thirty-two-year-old Harvey was very sad.

Although Harvey had been close with his mother, he had never really been close with his father or brother. His mother's death made things even worse. He didn't talk to or see much of his father or brother after that.

To make matters even worse, Harvey became bored at work. He decided to do what he always did when he didn't like where his life was going: move. He tried Puerto Rico first, but when he couldn't find work there, he went back to Miami, Florida. When that didn't work out, he moved back to New York and got a job doing research on Wall Street. The work may not have been exciting, but Harvey could afford fancy suits and another Manhattan apartment.

Although Harvey was good at his job, he didn't get along that well with most of his coworkers. He had very strong opinions, and he would let others know when he thought his way of doing something would work and theirs wouldn't. Harvey was usually right, but his coworkers didn't appreciate his I-told-you-so attitude.

Around 1964, Harvey met a theater director and composer named Tom O'Horgan and was introduced to a new way of life. Harvey kept his boring day job, but his nights were spent at the theater, and, sometimes, on the stage itself. The kid who had loved an audience turned into an adult who still loved having all eyes on him.

Harvey's new nightlife had a big impact on him. He let his hair grow long and grew a big mustache like his new friends had. When Tom O'Horgan was sent to San Francisco to work on a show, Harvey moved there in 1969, too. He loved the culture of the city. A lot of people there weren't afraid to show who they were in public. For a long time, Harvey thought it was safer to hide the fact that he was gay from his

family and work colleagues. But in San Francisco, he was beginning to change his mind.

When Harvey returned to New York again, it was only for a short time. He was now forty-one, and he felt like he needed to try something completely different. And he believed San Francisco was the place to do it. In 1972, Harvey moved there for good with his boyfriend, Scott Smith.

Scott and Harvey found an apartment in the Castro district—a neighborhood popular with San Francisco's gay community. They also adopted a dog they named The Kid. Now that they had solved the problem of where to live, they had to figure out where they would work.

In the days before digital photos appeared instantly on a smartphone screen, people used cameras loaded with film to take pictures. They sent or took their film to labs that developed the film and printed their photos. After a film store had ruined photos Harvey had taken of himself and Scott, Harvey thought he could do better. He would be more careful with other people's photos. He felt this was especially important for the people in the neighborhood because their pictures revealed a way of life not everyone accepted. Plus, he had the experience of working in the stores that his grandfather and father had owned.

Harvey and Scott opened Castro Camera on March 3, 1973, next door to where they lived on Castro Street.

Castro Camera wasn't much to look at. It wasn't big, and some people even described it as "dingy." The shop had an old, sagging red sofa and a barber's chair. There was a big counter with a gray curtain behind it that set apart an office space. The office had an old wooden desk, a fridge, and a coffee maker.

Music played in the store, and it was usually opera.

CHAPTER 6
Getting Political

One day, not long after he and Scott opened the store, a local government official came and told Harvey he had to pay one hundred dollars right away for a license to keep the store open. Harvey got angry with the man and refused,

sending him away. Harvey called the office responsible for licenses, and after spending many hours talking to many people, he was able to pay only thirty dollars for the license instead of one hundred. He was proud of his success, and told his friends.

Later, a teacher came into the store asking to rent a projector that she needed for a class lesson. The teacher told Harvey that the school had only a few projectors to share, and because they were so popular, the teachers had to wait a long time to get one. This teacher needed a projector right away. Harvey became angry that the city wasn't giving more money to schools.

Harvey brought a television into the store. He began watching the Watergate hearings, which began May 17, 1973. He watched, and yelled, as members of the US Senate interviewed President Richard Nixon and members of his

Republican staff. In 1972, a few people who worked on Nixon's reelection campaign had been caught breaking into the campaign headquarters of the opposite party, the Democratic National Committee, at the Watergate offices in Washington, DC. As the hearings got underway, the committee wanted to determine whether the president and his top staffers had known what was going on. The president was being asked about other "dirty tricks" he may have been involved in. The entire country was shocked. Just like Harvey, other viewers couldn't stop watching. But for Harvey, the scandal changed something deep inside him.

He wanted to do more to help solve problems, like the ones he learned about at the camera store. He thought the government wasn't doing enough to help people—or was doing the wrong things, like sending the official who had asked for one hundred dollars. Harvey also thought that if he was part of the government, he could help start to change things, especially for members of the gay community.

Just as Harvey used to keep the fact that he was gay a secret because he was afraid of losing his job, there were still many people being fired just for being gay, and many places that wouldn't even hire gay people. Harvey felt the government wasn't doing enough to protect them or their rights.

He decided to run for the position of city supervisor in 1973. City supervisors are members of the San Francisco Board of Supervisors, the organization responsible for making and changing laws for the city of San Francisco. There were five open spots on the board, and everyone in San Francisco could vote for any of the candidates. Those who got the most votes would win the five positions.

AT LAST **YOU** HAVE
A CANDIDATE FOR
SUPERVISOR
HARVEY
MILK
MILK MILK MILK
HAS SOMETHING FOR EVERYBODY

Castro Camera turned into Harvey's campaign headquarters. An artist named Tom Randol created posters. "Milk Has Something for Everybody," they read. Harvey's friends helped in any way they could.

In the front window of the store was a sign telling people to vote for Harvey, next to a photo of him with a mustache and hair pulled back in a ponytail. Harvey went all over the city, carrying campaign flyers and a box. He'd put the box on the ground and stand on it. Then, just as if he were on a stage, he'd loudly introduce himself and begin talking about what was important to him, and what his campaign stood for, as he handed out the flyers. Harvey wanted to make health care available to more people, and he wanted there to be less discrimination against gay people, and also against people of color.

His friends thought he might scare people with his long hair and casual clothes, but Harvey didn't want to look like a businessman again. He refused to cut his hair or shave his mustache.

Not everyone in San Francisco thought Harvey should be running for city office. Some believed gay candidates shouldn't say publicly that they were gay. They worried that the label might discourage straight supporters from voting for Harvey. But Harvey disagreed. He thought that being clear about their sexuality was a good way for gay people to become more accepted. If others saw gay people in positions of power, they would begin to respect them.

Harvey was worrying about another problem: He didn't have much money. Campaigns are expensive. Some candidates benefited from the wealthy people and powerful businesses that donated money to their campaigns. Harvey didn't want those kinds of donations. He believed they made candidates who got elected that way more likely to work harder for their donors than for the regular citizens they represented.

Harvey was especially popular with young people. He was even the favorite candidate of a local college. When Election Day came, on November 6, 1973, Harvey ended up with

seventeen thousand votes. It wasn't enough for him to win one of the five spots. In the end, Harvey came in tenth out of the thirty-two candidates who ran. Not bad for his first try. That's how Harvey saw it. It was his first time running for political office but not his last.

Gay and Lesbian Rights in the United States

When Harvey was growing up, many gay men and lesbian women kept their same-sex relationships a secret from their families, friends, and employers. They were afraid of being fired from or unable to get a job. They were afraid their families and friends would not accept them. In most states, it was a crime to be gay. That began  to slowly change during the 1950s. Gay rights groups like the Mattachine Society were created, publicly calling for changes to the way society treated gay people.

The gay rights movement grew stronger throughout the 1960s, inspired by the civil rights movement, which called for fair and equal treatment of African Americans. In 1969, after police raided the Stonewall Inn, a gay bar in the Greenwich Village neighborhood of New York City, and arrested some of the people there, the gay community decided to fight back. This became known as the Stonewall riots. It was considered the beginning of the modern gay rights movement.

Slowly, change happened. In 2009, committing a crime against someone because of their sexual orientation or gender identity became defined as a hate crime. In 2015, a Supreme Court ruling made same-sex marriage legal throughout the United States.

CHAPTER 7
The Mayor of Castro Street

Not long after the election, a man named Allan Baird entered Castro Camera. Allan was a straight man who had grown up in the Castro. He worked with the Teamsters, a labor union. A union is a group of workers who join forces to ask for better pay and working conditions. (Sometimes, companies don't want to sign contracts with unions.)

The Teamsters

The International Brotherhood of Teamsters was started in 1903. At first, the Teamsters was a union formed to represent drivers. The union would work with individuals or companies that employ people, to negotiate salaries and benefits, like health care, for its members. The union signs a contract with the employer so that every union member who is hired gets the same kinds of benefits. Today, there 1.4 million union members, and they are not just drivers. The Teamsters represents groups from pilots and police officers to secretaries and construction workers.

Allan was working on a boycott against six beer companies that didn't want to hire union drivers. People who participate in a boycott hope to send a strong message by refusing to buy certain products or go to certain places. In this case, Allan was trying to get businesses to stop accepting beer deliveries from the companies that wouldn't hire union drivers. He already had gotten organizations of Arab and Chinese grocery store owners to agree not to sell the beer in their stores. Allan also wanted gay-owned bars to join the boycott, and he thought Harvey could help with that plan.

Harvey decided to make a deal with Allan Baird. He would help convince owners of gay bars to participate if Allan let gay people join the union so they could get jobs as drivers.

Harvey wanted to make it known that the gay community was an important group of people who spent money at businesses in San Francisco.

If the larger community didn't start paying attention, it might lose them as customers. Having the gay community join the boycott would help Harvey prove his idea.

At the time, there were about a hundred gay-
and lesbian-owned bars in the area. Harvey and
his friends went to all of them, asking them to
be part of the beer boycott. Harvey convinced
reporters to follow him, and he turned the
encounters into a real show. TV reporters took
videos of owners removing bottles from their

bars in protest, until the beer companies changed their minds about hiring only nonunion drivers. Soon, they did—all the companies except for Coors signed contracts with the union. Coors refused, and had to deal with selling a lot less beer in San Francisco.

And Allan kept his word. Gay drivers were let into the Teamsters union, and soon, companies were hiring them. Allan also gave Harvey a gift: a bullhorn, like the one he used to rally union crowds. Now, Harvey wouldn't have to stand  on top of a box and yell to be heard.

Harvey's partnership with the Teamsters proved that he could work with all kinds of people and groups in San Francisco. It also showed that San Francisco's gay community had the power to enact change.

As Harvey prepared for his second race to become a city supervisor, he decided he had to make some changes to his image. He cut his hair and shaved off his mustache. Scott didn't like doing so, but he helped Harvey shop for a suit and some button-down shirts. Harvey hoped the new look would make more people take him seriously.

In the mid-1970s, Harvey got a nickname: the mayor of Castro Street. No one knew for sure whether someone started calling him that or Harvey made up the moniker himself. Either way, reporters began using that nickname in their stories.

By that time, Castro Camera had a reputation as a place to go if you were new to the city and didn't quite know what to do. Harvey helped people find places to live and work. He'd also tell them to register to vote. Castro Camera felt like home to many in the neighborhood. For regulars and first-time visitors alike, it was a good spot for anyone seeking advice or just a friendly chat.

In 1975, Castro Camera was filled with volunteers and campaign workers. People would walk in and Harvey would learn about their lives and give them jobs. There was something about Harvey that made people excited to be around him.

Medora Payne, an eleven-year-old Catholic schoolgirl, turned up one day to volunteer. When Harvey's campaign manager called her parents to make sure it was okay for her to be there, they told him she was a big fan of Harvey! She had been asking to volunteer for a long time. Medora soon became a familiar face at Castro Camera.

Even though he lost a few elections, Harvey got more and more votes each time he ran. He also got many more groups—in addition to the gay community—to support him, including women's rights groups, black political groups, environmental groups, unions, and others.

CHAPTER 8
Victory at Last

In January 1976, a new mayor, George Moscone, took office in San Francisco. Harvey liked George and had worked to get him elected. Harvey thought George would fight for gay people's rights. He had already helped change one law against gays

George Moscone

when he was state senator. And George liked Harvey—enough to offer him a position in city government that year, on the Board of Permit Appeals. The Board of Permit Appeals is the office responsible for granting special permission to tackle projects like constructing new buildings.

Harvey took the job, but it lasted just over a month because he decided to run for office again—this time for the California State Assembly. He lost the election but not by much.

And that wasn't the only thing Harvey lost at the time. Scott had never been happy about Harvey's attempts to be a politician, even though he helped with the campaigns. Scott had always imagined a different life for them. And so he broke up with Harvey.

There was still one election looming for Harvey in 1977: his third attempt to land a spot on the San Francisco Board of Supervisors. That year, there was a change in the election process. Harvey didn't need to get the entire city's vote. Instead, he needed just the support of his district—and the Castro was a big part of that.

On election night, Harvey won his district with 30 percent of the vote. There had been

sixteen other candidates, but it was Harvey who would become a city supervisor. When Harvey, who had been awaiting the results at city hall, arrived by motorcycle at Castro Camera, the crowd that had gathered there went wild. Someone gave him a bottle of champagne, and Harvey, who didn't drink, poured it over his own head. The celebration continued.

Kathy Kozachenko

Before Harvey's win, there had been only a few openly gay people elected to public office anywhere in the country. The two most notable were the lesbian politicians Kathy Kozachenko, who was elected to the city council in Ann Arbor, Michigan, in 1974, and Elaine Noble, elected in 1975 to the Massachusetts House of Representatives for the first of two terms. Harvey became the first person running as an openly gay man to be elected in the United States.

Elaine Noble

Newspapers throughout the country wrote about his victory. Harvey received very personal congratulations as well. His brother, Robert, sent him a letter that began: "Dear Mr. Supervisor . . ."

CHAPTER 9
In Office

Harvey was officially sworn into office on the board of supervisors on January 9, 1978. He knew that newspaper and television photographers would be there to cover the event because he was making history.

So Harvey asked to have an outdoor swearing-in ceremony. He wanted San Francisco City Hall in the background of all the pictures. To get there, he and a group of 150 supporters walked fifteen blocks from Castro Camera.

Right from the start, Harvey worked hard as a supervisor. He wanted to learn all the facts before he voted. He let people know that he was going to think for himself. He'd vote for the ideas that would become the laws that were most helpful to the people of San Francisco. He wasn't concerned whether those laws were popular with the other supervisors. Harvey tried hard to make sure poor people and older people all over the city had affordable places to live. He also wanted to make sure that new homes that were being built weren't too expensive. In addition, Harvey saved a school and a library in his district from being closed.

Harvey Milk and Dan White

A number of new people were elected to the board of supervisors at the same time as Harvey. One of them was Dan White. In many ways, Harvey and Dan were very different. Dan was a former police officer. The two men appeared together in a lot of interviews. But Harvey and Dan got along. Harvey thought that even though they disagreed about some things, they were both interested in helping their communities.

Harvey and Dan struck a deal with each other. Dan helped make sure the entire board would vote on a gay rights bill that Harvey wanted to pass. In exchange, Harvey agreed to support Dan's cause. Dan White was against an idea to build a new center in his district for young people who had committed crimes. Dan thought it would be bad for the people living in his district.

Harvey agreed with Dan at first and was going to vote against the plan. But he changed his mind. He learned that the center would be a place for kids who otherwise would have to be sent to live far from their families. Harvey voted *for* the plan, and it passed.

Dan was really angry. He didn't speak to Harvey for months. He began voting against any idea that Harvey proposed.

While Harvey was in office, a proposal for a new law—called a proposition—was put up for a vote in the state of California. If enough people voted yes, it would become law. Proposition 6 was introduced by John Briggs, a state senator. He wanted to prevent gay people from working in public schools in California.

Harvey thought this was a terrible idea. When he had been a teacher, he had been afraid of being fired for being gay. Harvey did everything he could to make sure Proposition 6 failed. He appeared on television to speak out against it. Everywhere John Briggs went to promote the bill,

John Briggs

Harvey followed, arguing against it. They had debates on TV, with Harvey making logical and passionate arguments.

On June 25, 1978, Harvey stood in front of a gigantic crowd, wearing jeans, a white T-shirt, and a giant necklace of pink and white flowers. It was San Francisco's Gay Freedom Day Parade, and Harvey had something to say. He began: "My name's Harvey Milk—and I want to recruit you."

The "Hope" Speech

In the late 1970s, many cities across the country were getting rid of gay rights laws that gay activists had worked so hard to put in place. Harvey wanted to give young people something to look forward to, a way to believe that their future would get better despite the dark times.

"You have to give them hope," he said. Harvey believed that if people helped elect him, it would mean "hope to a nation that has given up, because if a gay person makes it, the doors are open to everyone."

Harvey wanted more gay people to run for office. He said they would serve as role models who would let other lesbian and gay people, especially young people, know that things could get better.

Proposition 6 was defeated on November 7, 1978—by more than one million votes.

CHAPTER 10
A Sad Day in San Francisco

Ten months after the new supervisors had been sworn into office, Dan White resigned. Supervisors weren't paid a lot of money, so it was difficult to have just that one job. And Dan did *not* like losing. He got really upset when votes didn't go his way.

But then, Dan's supporters began to tell him his resignation was a mistake. They told him to try to get his job back. Dan went to Mayor Moscone and asked to become a supervisor again. The mayor told him the board had already accepted his letter of resignation, but he would see what might be done about Dan's request.

Harvey, however, had already suggested the names of people to take Dan's place—

candidates who would help pass the kinds of bills Harvey and the mayor wanted to enact. Harvey especially wanted someone who supported the gay community. He convinced the mayor not to reinstate Dan.

When Dan found out—from a reporter—that he wasn't getting his job back, he was extremely angry. On November 27, 1978, the day Dan's replacement as the new supervisor was going to be announced, Dan snuck into city hall through a window. He had a gun hidden under his jacket.

He went to see the mayor and, when they were alone, Dan shot him. He then went to find Harvey. He shot him, too. Dan ran away and called his wife to tell her what he had done. She went with him to the police station so that he could confess to the murders of Harvey Milk and Mayor George Moscone.

Harvey Milk died in city hall. He was forty-eight years old.

City Hall Murders

MOSCONE, MILK SLAIN --DAN WHITE IS HELD

San Francisco Chronicle

Mayor
Was Hit
4 Times

Feinstein Becomes the Mayor

When Dianne Feinstein, who was the president of the board of supervisors at the time, announced that Mayor Moscone and Harvey Milk had been killed, everyone was shocked and sad—including Ms. Feinstein herself—as she delivered the news.

Dianne Feinstein

Dianne Feinstein (1933–)

Dianne Feinstein was born and raised in San Francisco. She was first elected to the San Francisco Board of Supervisors in 1969, and was reelected  two times, continuing to serve until 1978. After Mayor Moscone was murdered, she became the temporary mayor of San Francisco, which made her the city's first woman mayor. She was officially elected mayor in November 1979 and then reelected in 1983, serving in that office until 1988.

Dianne Feinstein was first elected as a senator representing California in the US Congress in 1992. She and Barbara Boxer, also elected to the US Congress in 1992, became the first two women elected as senators from California.

That evening, San Franciscans from every neighborhood came to Castro Street, carrying candles. Then, in a procession of tens of thousands of people, led by three men carrying the US, California, and San Francisco flags, they marched silently toward city hall, candles lit.

The governor of California, Jerry Brown, ordered all flags in the state to be flown at half-mast. He said that Harvey had been a hardworking "leader of San Francisco's gay community." The next day, the *San Francisco Examiner* headline read: "A City in Agony."

When Dan White went on trial in early May 1979, he was found guilty but was given a maximum sentence of only seven years in jail. It was a short sentence for a man who had killed two people.

After the jury's decision was announced on May 21, a crowd gathered in the Castro, much as one had on the day when Harvey was sworn in. But this time, the people were angry. They, too, marched to city hall. Once there, many of the protestors started breaking whatever they could: car windows, the sidewalk. Some broke off tree branches and set them on fire. The march had turned into a series of violent riots. They became known as the White Night riots, referring to Dan White's name. The next day, May 22, 1979, would have been Harvey's forty-ninth birthday.

Even though Harvey's life ended tragically, and even though he spent less than a year in office, people still remember Harvey and what he was able to accomplish in such a short time. He was one of the first openly gay people in the country to run for and win an elected position. While in office, he fought hard against Proposition 6 and won. Because of his efforts, openly gay teachers in California could work without fear of being fired because of their sexuality.

Harvey's work and life continue to inspire others. His story was made into the Oscar-winning movie *Milk*, starring Sean Penn, and an opera, *Harvey Milk*. There is even a US postage stamp that honors Harvey.

A high school for LGBTQ+ teens in New York City is named after him. Harvey Milk Public High School welcomes gay, lesbian, bisexual, and transgender students, as well as those who question their sexual identity.

What does *LGBTQ+* stand for?

The term *LGB* stands for *Lesbian*, *Gay*, and *Bisexual*. It replaced the term *gay* in the 1980s. In the 1990s, it grew to include *T* for *Transgender*, as in *LGBT*.

Currently, the term *LGBTQ+* is used to refer to the diversity of sexuality and gender identity.

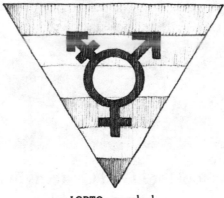

LGBTQ+ symbol

The *Q* stands for *Queer* or *Questioning*, and the *+* stands for all the people who feel that none of these terms fully defines or describes them.

Because of Harvey's military service, a US Navy ship will proudly carry his name; it will be called the USNS *Harvey Milk*.

In California, there is now an official Harvey Milk Day, celebrated May 22, to remember and honor Harvey on his birthday, and in 2009, President Barack Obama awarded the Presidential Medal of Freedom to Harvey.

Harvey Milk's nephew receives the Presidential Medal of Freedom on behalf of his uncle.

The description of the award, which is the highest civilian honor in the United States, said that Harvey's election "changed the landscape of opportunity for the nation's gay community."

The example Harvey set continues to inspire others to act. In his "Hope" speech, Harvey said that "if a gay person can be elected, it's a green light." Since his death, openly gay and lesbian people have been elected to Congress and the Senate. People in cities across the country have voted for gay and lesbian mayors, and recently, the first openly gay governor. Thanks to Harvey Milk, the present looks more like the future he hoped for.

Timeline of Harvey Milk's Life

1930	Harvey Bernard Milk is born in Woodmere, New York, on May 22
1947	Graduates from Bay Shore High School
1951	Graduates from the New York State College for Teachers
	Joins the US Navy
1956	Meets Joe Campbell, starts a job as a high school teacher
1962	Harvey's mother, Minnie, dies
1972	Moves to San Francisco with Scott Smith
1973	Opens Castro Camera with Scott
	Runs (and loses) for the first time for a spot on the San Francisco Board of Supervisors
1974	Helps the Teamsters with a boycott of beer distributors in the Castro neighborhood of San Francisco
1975	Runs (and loses) again for the board of supervisors
1976	San Francisco mayor George Moscone names Harvey to the Board of Permit Appeals
1977	Runs for the board of supervisors a third time and wins
1978	Gives what is now called the "Hope" speech
	Speaks out against Proposition 6 in California
	Assassinated by Dan White, on November 27
2009	California recognizes May 22 as Harvey Milk Day

Timeline of the World

1930 — The *Mickey Mouse* comic strip first appears in US newspapers

1939 — World War II begins in September

1945 — World War II ends, on September 2

1953 — The coronation of Queen Elizabeth II takes place in Westminster Abbey, London, England

1963 — Martin Luther King Jr. delivers his "I Have a Dream" speech at the March on Washington, in Washington, DC

1964 — South African anti-apartheid leader Nelson Mandela is sent to prison

1967 — Thurgood Marshall is confirmed as the first African American Supreme Court justice

1969 — Hundreds of thousands of people gather and dozens of music groups perform at the Woodstock music festival

— The Stonewall Riots, in response to a police raid on a gay bar in New York City, lead to the beginning of the gay rights movement

1971 — Walt Disney World Resort opens near Orlando, Florida

1973 — Billie Jean King beats Bobby Riggs in a tennis match known as the Battle of the Sexes

1978 — Mavis Hutchison becomes the first woman to run across the United States

Bibliography

*Books for young readers

Chan, Sewell. "Film Evokes Memories for Milk's Relatives," *New York Times*, February 20, 2009.

Faderman, Lillian. *Harvey Milk: His Lives and Death.* New Haven, CT: Yale University Press, 2018.

Leyland, Winston, ed. *Out in the Castro: Desire, Promise, Activism.* San Francisco, CA: Leyland Publications, 2002.

Milk, Harvey. *An Archive of Hope: Harvey Milk's Speeches and Writings.* Edited by Jason Edward Black and Charles E. Morris III. Berkeley, CA: University of California Press, 2013.

Milk, Harvey. *The Harvey Milk Interviews: In His Own Words.* Edited by Vince Emery. San Francisco, CA: Vince Emery Productions, 2012.

*Sanders, Rob. *Pride: The Story of Harvey Milk and the Rainbow Flag.* Illustrated by Steven Salerno. New York: Random House, 2018.

Shilts, Randy. *The Mayor of Castro Street: The Life and Times of Harvey Milk.* New York: St. Martin's Press, 1978.

Website

www.milkfoundation.org